T0114747

THE LIFE OF DR WYSON MOSES

KAUZOBAFA JELE

Published by

Mzuni Press

P/Bag 201 Luwinga

Mzuzu 2

ISBN 978-99960-60-48-9

eISBN 978-99960-60-47-2

The Mzuni Press is represented outside Africa by:

African Books Collective Oxford

(order@africanbookscollective.com)

www.africanbookscollective.com

www.mzunipress.blogspot.com

Printed in Malawi by Baptist Publications, P.O. Box 444, Lilongwe

The Life of Dr. Wyson Moses Kauzobafa Jele

Missionary to Zambia

Kelly Bwalya

Mzuni Press

Mzuni Books no. 14

Mzuzu
2017

Dedication

I dedicate this book to my lovely wife Dorcas Katyetye and our daughter Chazipa Bwalya who have been so patient during the time I was doing my final editing of this book.

Acknowledgements

First and foremost, I would like to thank God for the guidance and wisdom in getting this book into print. Furthermore, many colleagues gave their time and insights to the development of this book. Primarily, I wish to express my warm thanks to Rev Dr Wyson Moses Kauzobafa Jele for accepting my request to write a brief history of his life and work, which is not usual in the African context. I wish also to thank him for the kindness and hospitality he gave me, not only as an author but also as one of the products of his leadership. This outstanding opportunity was granted to me among many who longed to write about his life and work in Zambia. During this time, he was busy caring for his wife, NyaNhlane, who was very sick by then, but he spared time so that I could have a personal interview with him. Unfortunately, she passed on in 2011.

Sincerely, I also want to appreciate the constructive criticism of those who tirelessly responded to the drafts and helped me to improve it through the many helpful suggestions to this book.

Many thanks also go to the CCAP Synod offices of Livingstonia and Zambia for their encouragement and support and friends in Zambia and Malawi. All I could say is thank you and may the good Lord richly bless you. I also extend my gratitude to all my extended family members for their unceasing support during my final editing to this book. I would like to thank you, Mr. and Mrs. L. Gondwe and my sister Chanda Namukwayi (Mrs Lesa) for financial support. May the good Lord richly bless you and your families.

Rev Dr Jele (left) with the author, Rev Kelly Bwalya.

Abbreviations

BSZ	Bible Society of Zambia
CCAP	Church of Central Africa, Presbyterian
CCZ	Council of Churches in Zambia
CRCSA	Council of Reformed Churches in Southern Africa
CYF	Christian Youth Fellowship
EFM	Evangelical Fellowship in Malawi
EAM	Evangelical Association of Malawi
GAC	General Administration Committee
LMS	London Missionary Society
MCP	Malawi Congress Party
PCA	Presbyterian Church of Australia
PCI	Presbyterian Church in Ireland
RCZ	Reformed Church in Zambia
REC	Reformed Ecumenical Council
RSA	Republic of South Africa
TEEZ	Theological Education by Extension in Zambia
T/A	Traditional Authority
UK	United Kingdom
UPCSA	Uniting Presbyterian Church of Zambia
PC (USA)	Presbyterian Church in United Sates of America
WEF	World Evangelical Fellowship

Preface

This book explores the life and work of Rev Dr W.M.K. Jele, and his contribution to the Church of Central Africa Presbyterian, Synod of Zambia (CCAP). Jele served the CCAP Synod of Zambia from 1981 to 1988. From 1984 to 1988 he served as the first General Secretary of CCAP Synod of Zambia. The CCAP, Synod of Zambia traces its origin from the Free Church of Scotland. Since the 1880s it was known as the Free Church of Scotland of the Livingstonia Mission now CCAP Synod of Livingstonia. Its growth and development before 1984 depended on the missionaries from Scotland and CCAP Synod of Livingstonia in Malawi who could send missionaries to preach and administer the sacraments to the people of Northern Rhodesia, now Zambia. This was until 28 October 1984, when the CCAP in Zambia was given the status of a Synod by the CCAP General Assembly.

Documenting Jele's life and work in Zambia will help the upcoming young leaders to develop leadership skills for the continuation of church growth and development. The study of Jele's leadership style will be instrumental in enhancing the growth of the church not only in Zambia but also in other parts of Central Africa, and Africa as a continent. Studying leadership skills of our forerunners shapes our future and the future of the Church; it can also help the church to respond to the needs of the society which it is called to serve. The study contends that good leadership is one that enables others to be leaders. It demonstrates that Jele was a leader called to make others to be outstanding leaders. It further urges future leaders to emulate him. A good leader, according to this study, is one who is broadminded, principled, values delegation and is ecumenical.

This book is based on a thesis first submitted in partial fulfillment of the requirements for the Bachelor of Theology Degree in Church History at the College of Theology, University of Livingstonia under the supervision of the Rev W.K.L. Mumba on 24 March, 2010. It has been edited and prepared for publication by my good friend, the Very Rev Dr Bob Thomas, former Moderator General of the Presbyterian Church in Australia and Editor of New Life Christian Newspaper, as well as by Professor Klaus Fiedler, lecturer at Mzuzu University and editor of Mzuni Press.

Kelly Bwalya, 2017

CONTENT

INTRODUCTION

This book aims at providing the historical perspective of Dr Jele's life and contribution to the CCAP Synod of Zambia during the time he was a Parish Minister and General Secretary. Thus, this book's aim is to help shape future leaders to become visionary, creative and innovative, and able to help the church in evangelism, leadership training, administration, pastoral care, stewardship and accountability. As Charles Lindbergh said "success is not measured by what a man accomplishes, but by the opposition he encountered, and the courage he maintained in his struggle against it." Thus, this tells us that Jele's success is not in what he accomplished or did in his leadership style, but the opposition and the courage he had gone through which made him to go on. In short, persistence, courage, determination, desire, dedication and discipline are needed in whatever we do so that God will be with us throughout our daily living. Thus, all successes and challenges Jele experienced will become the strengths of the church and our lives.

Testimonial of this Book

History and leadership are two of the most important aspects in the life of the Church. Therefore, this book will examine and explore the life and work of the Rev Dr Wyson Kauzobafa Jele during the period he served the CCAP Synod of Zambia. It is a fact that success of any given institution, to some extent, is dependent on the kind of leadership style of the one leading it. If the institution has good leadership, there is a high possibility for it to succeed. Often poor leadership has led institutions to collapse. However, the suggestion being made is not that a leader can make any difference without the collaborative effort from those he is working with. Rather the contribution being made is that good leadership is the best tool to the great success of any institution. This applies to the church Jele led. The CCAP Synod of Zambia's success story, largely, is attributed to the life of one man, whose name is Rev Dr W.M.K. Jele, not as an individual but as a leader who worked through others. Jele's influence on the Zambian church remains so enormous that it needed some kind of study and documentation.

However, there is no written document about his life nor was a statue built in his memory. Though Silas Nyirenda and Victor Chilenje have written about the history of the Synod of Zambia, there is insignificant material concerning the role played by Jele, although he is mentioned in the history of CCAP in Zambia. It is becoming a tradition in the field of history to write an account of the leader who pioneered the leadership of any institution from an African perspective. Silas S. Ncozana has written the biography of Jonathan D. Sangaya, the first African General Secretary of Blantyre Synod of CCAP.[1] Surprisingly, the work of Ncozana has been incorporated as a recommended text in the Syllabus of Malawian Theological Colleges. What is interesting is not that it is one of the recommended texts but that Sangaya is considered as a model for future leaders of the church. It is against this background that I would like to explore and examine the life and work of Rev Dr Jele in the Synod of Zambia. Let me say about Dr Jele as Silas S. Ncozana has written about Sangaya:

> We indeed remember Sangaya, as a soldier for Christ … after he had faithfully served his Master and his fellow human beings … Let us strive in our pilgrimage of faith and service to follow the example of people like Sangaya.[2]

What is fascinating is the appeal that Ncozana makes. This is the reason that has prompted this book to re-examine the legacy of Jele in the Zambian context of the CCAP family. Studying Jele's life and work in Zambia will help the upcoming young leaders to develop their leadership skills for the continued growth and development of the church. The study of Jele's contribution through his leadership style will be instrumental in enhancing the growth of the church, not only in Zambia but also in other parts of Central Africa, and Africa as a continent. Studying leadership skills of our forerunners not only shapes our future and the future of the church; it also helps the church to respond to the needs of society to which it is called to serve. Furthermore, the approach Jele used as a leader will enable the church in Zambia to examine and reconsider its leadership style and approach.

While some scholars have written on other leaders, this book is specifically about Dr Jele because of his unique contribution to the church

---

[1]   Silas S. Ncozana, *Sangaya, A Leader in the Synod of Blantyre Church of Central Africa Presbyterian*, Blantyre: CLAIM-Kachere, 1999, p. 58.

[2]   Ibid.

in Zambia. The study on the life and work of Dr Jele will help the Church also to reread its history and redefine it in some areas it has failed to do well in remembering those who have made profound contributions to the church.

Another reason that necessitated the writing of this book on the life and contribution of Jele is the way the Zambian CCAP members hold him in respect. The members of the CCAP Synod of Zambia have not forgotten Jele because of the rapid change that he brought while serving them as leader-servant. It is now almost 25 years since the CCAP Synod of Zambia became an autonomous church and about 21 years since Dr Jele left Zambia, but people still regard him as one of the most outstanding leaders among many who laboured with him in the church of Zambia. Most of those interviewed said Jele's contributions came in as a result of his visionary leadership by making right priorities such as a quality educational system of teaching the members in the church, initiating development projects based on the philosophy advocated by Henry Venn, to make the church self-supporting, self-propagating and self-governing.[3]

What inspired me to write this book?

While I was in Lusaka, some members of the CCAP used to say that our success as a Synod depended on the leadership of Jele. At the time he was leaving Zambia, many members cried, not necessarily that he was leaving but remembering how useful he had been to them in all aspects of life. His leaving created a great gap because Zambia expected him to leave after grooming more leaders who could take over from him. They said Jele knew where he was taking the church. Additionally, when I was in Lundazi at David McConaughey's congregation, I found that there is a Section named Dr Jele. However, this is still insignificant as a way of remembering him compared to what he did for the church. Above all, this was a local arrangement by the congregation, but I felt that something needed to be done at Synod level. Thus, enthusiasm raised the curiosity to know more about this man and his leadership skills. These questions and many more led me to want to study the life of this man. A quick survey showed that the man had done a lot for the church, but that it had not

---

[3]   David Bosch, *Transforming Mission*, Maryknoll, New York: Orbis Books, 1991, p. 307.

been documented. The result of this survey was an in-depth study of his life and work in Zambia.

Method used in writing this book

This book is a historical inquiry into the life and work of Rev Dr W.M.K. Jele. Since the book focuses on the life and work of Jele as a leader in the Synod of Zambia, interviews were conducted in both Malawi and Zambia. The interviews were either through a questionnaire or personal interviews which targeted a cross-section of Christians, both clergy and laity, who worked with Jele. Thus, a list of questions was sent to some selected persons who knew and worked with Rev Dr Jele in Malawi and Zambia. While doing this, I had the opportunity to have a one to one interview with the Dr Jele at his home village Etchiyeni near Mzimba Boma and in Mzuzu. In addition, questionnaires were sent to individuals in Lusaka and Lundazi from the age of thirty years and above. Also, being one of the church ministers of the CCAP Synod of Zambia who benefited much from Dr Jele's contributions, I will contribute what I feel is significant from my own perspective. However, this will not obstruct what others have said.

Historical Background of CCAP Synod of Zambia

The Church of Central African Presbyterian Synod of Zambia traces its origin from the Free Church of Scotland, which had covered the northern part of the Central Region and Northern Region of Malawi as well as some parts of Eastern and Northern Zambia before it expanded to the whole country of Zambia. This tells us that the CCAP in Zambia is within the context of the wider family of the Church of Central Africa Presbyterian, which was established in 1924 by Livingstonia and Blantyre Presbyteries and was joined in 1926 by Nkhoma Mission of the Dutch Reformed Church. Then Harare CCAP Synod in Zimbabwe followed in 1965, while the CCAP Synod of Zambia joined in 1984.[4] Therefore, "the CCAP family consists of five regional Synods from three countries united in a General Assembly with its administrative office in Lilongwe, Malawi."[5] The Livingstonia Mission was

---

[4] Victor Chilenje, The Origin and Development of the Church of Central Africa Presbyterian in Zambia 1882-2004, PhD, Stellenbosch University, p. 1
[5] Ibid.

the first mission to be established in 1875 by the Free Church of Scotland when "on 18th October 1875, the first tent of Livingstonia was erected" at Cape Maclear.[6] The second station was established at Bandawe in 1881 because there were few inhabitants at Cape Maclear.[7] After the station was moved to Bandawe, more stations were opened in Malawi, especially in the Northern Region and some parts of the Central Region. This "work was also extended to some parts of Northern Rhodesia (Zambia) giving birth to the CCAP Synod of Livingstonia in 1956 and eventually, the CCAP Synod of Zambia in 1984."[8] This is why CCAP Synod of Zambia's growth and development before 1984 depended on the missionaries from Scotland and CCAP Livingstonia Mission in Malawi who sent missionaries to be pastors there to preach and administer the sacraments to the people of Northern Rhodesia, now Zambia. This went on until 28 October 1984, when the CCAP in Zambia was given the status of a Synod.[9] As evidenced by Chilenje that "from 1956 – 1984 the Livingstonia Mission work had continued in Zambia by the CCAP Synod of Livingstonia, a product of the Livingstonia Mission and the local Zambian people."[10]

Livingstonia Mission had, until 1968, three Presbyteries. These were Livingstonia-Karonga Presbytery in the north, which covered Rumphi and Karonga/Chitipa districts and Northern Province of Zambia; Ekwendeni-Bandawe Presbytery in the central region, which covered Mzimba North, Nkhata Bay/Nkhotakota districts and Loudon-Chasefu Presbytery in the south which covered Mzimba South, parts of the Central Region of Malawi and the Eastern Province of Northern Rhodesia, now Zambia.

However, the suggestion here is not that the Synod of Zambia was constituted by Loudon-Chasefu Presbytery, as a matter of procedure in the CCAP policy; it is the prerogative of the General Assembly to establish another Synod apart from the existing Synods. The Loudon-Chasefu Presbytery is referred to as the root of the Synod of Zambia. This is because Loudon-Chasefu had been operating in Zambia as part of the Livingstonia Mission Presbytery from the 1880s until Chasefu was constituted a Presbytery in 1975. The Livingstonia-Karonga Presbytery supervised some

---

[6] E.D. Young, *Mission to Nyassa, a Journal of Adventures*. John Murray. London: 1877, p. 77.
[7] Robert Laws, *Reminiscences of Livingstonia*, Edinburgh: Oliver and Boyd, 1934, p. 85.
[8] Victor Chilenje, *PhD Thesis*, p. 2
[9] Interview Dr Jele, Etchiyeni village, Mphongo, 20.5.2009.
[10] Victor Chilenje, *PhD Thesis*, p. iii.

parts of the Northern Province of Zambia and established Lubwa, Mwenzo and Chitambo mission stations.[11] Thus, Livingstonia was the first established Church to work in Malawi and in some parts of Zambia.

In the Northern Province of Zambia, the work continued in Muyombe and in the Eastern Province, the work continued in Chama, Lundazi and some parts of Chipata. Apart from the fact that the people in these districts did not want to lose their Presbyterian heritage, there was something more that attached the people in these districts to the people in Malawi. The people of the Northern part of Zambia, particularly those in Nakonde, Isoka and Muyombe Districts and those in the Eastern part of Zambia like Chama, Lundazi and Chipata share a common language and culture with the people of Mzimba, Rumphi, and Chitipa in Malawi. Their chiefs were related and the people had intermarried, thereby forming a very strong bond of family relationships.

However, the Synod of Livingstonia had some difficulties in running the Church in Zambia because the catchment's area was so vast. Travelling was expensive and risky as people had to walk long distances on foot and risked their lives to the wild animals, tsetse flies, crossing big rivers and other hazardous conditions, especially in Malambo Valley.[12] Hence a committee was formed by the General Assembly to assess whether a Synod could be constituted. After the presentation of the report, it was agreed that a Synod be constituted in Zambia. This is briefly how the Synod of Zambia was constituted. Its birth impressed all members of the CCAP General Assembly as indicated in minute no 6 of the CCAP General Synod meeting held at Ekwendeni in 1987. This minute says, "The Moderator of the General Synod, the Right Rev Dr S.S. Ncozana, welcomed this newly constituted CCAP Synod of Zambia whose presence testifies to the growth of CCAP spiritually, numerically and in its witness."[13] After the inauguration, the Rev Dr Wyson Jele, a Malawian, was elected as the first General Secretary of CCAP Synod of Zambia together with other office bearers who were indigenous Zambian clergy and laity, as we will see later. This book will evaluate the contribution of Rev Dr Wyson Jele to the growth of the CCAP in Zambia.

From a missiological perspective, Jele can be described as a missionary to the Zambian community if the word missionary is defined as someone

---

[11] J. Weller & J. Linden, *Mainstream Christianity to 1980 in Malawi, Zambia and Zimbabwe*, Gweru: Mambo Press, 1984, p. 148.
[12] Interview Rev S.M. Mithi, 14.7.2009.
[13] Minutes of the General Synod, 1987, p. 30.

commissioned by his church to work with an autonomous church of the same family with the same doctrines in another country. The CCAP Synod of Zambia at the time Jele became its General Secretary was an autonomous Synod from the Livingstonia Synod, to which he was a missionary.

As a member of the Presbyterian family, the CCAP Synod of Zambia subscribes to the Westminster Confession of faith, the Heidelberg Catechism, the Lager Catechism and Shorter Catechism.

Zambia Synod is a member of the Reformed Ecumenical Council. The CCAP General Synod is also a member of the World Alliance of Reformed Churches. Locally Zambia Synod is a member of the Evangelical Fellowship of Zambia (EFZ), the Christian Council of Zambia (CCZ), Theological Education by Extension in Zambia (TEEZ) and the Bible Society (BSZ).

Furthermore, the Church has close relations with the Reformed Church of Zambia (RCZ), the United Church of Zambia (UCZ) and the Uniting Presbyterian Church of Zambia (UPCSA). The CCAP Synod of Zambia carries on a missionary witness by having organized preaching stations (prayer houses) and local evangelists at congregational level, and it has presbytery evangelists at the Presbytery level. They also organize evangelism out-reach campaigns with the help of the men's guild, women's guild and youth who are known as the Christian Youth Fellowship (CYF).

CHAPTER ONE: KNOWING AND EXPLORING JELE AS AN INDIVIDUAL

Rev Dr Jele when he was 83 years old in August 2012 at Synod meeting in Zambia

Birth and Early Childhood

Wyson Moses Kauzobafa Jele was born on 15 December 1929 in Etchiyeni village in Mphongo area T/A M'mbelwa, Mzimba district. Jele's father was Moses Sunduzwayo Jele. His mother, Nelly Mafunase Mzoma Nhlane, was a granddaughter of Mayayi Chiputula Nhlane,[14] "the first Ngoni chief to meet the Livingstonia Mission in 1877."[15] The time Wyson was born, his parents were both church elders of the Loudon-Chasefu Presbytery. Nelly Nhlane's Christian life can be traced to the time her grandfather Chiputula Nhlane invited the Livingstonia Mission in 1877. This formed a good background for Jele's Christian life. Consequently, he was baptized as an infant by the Rev Andrew Mkochi and was

---

[14] Interview Dr Jele, Etchiyeni village, Mphongo, 20.5.2009.

[15] T. Jack Thompson, *Christianity in Northern Malawi*, Leiden: Brill, 1995, p. 107.

confirmed to full church membership by Rev Lameck Ngozi Mvula in September 1948.[16]

Jele comes from a family of two boys. He was the youngest, and his elder brother was a minister in the National African Church.[17] As a youth, Jele learned all the skills required of any Ngoni boy, such as farming and hunting, and he developed a spirit of sharing. He was a good *mliska wa mbuzi na ng'ombe* (shepherd of goats and cattle) for his father's animals and those of his grandparents. Shepherding goats and cattle requires patience, perseverance and caring. This may have helped Jele to develop into the kind of a leader that he was.

Jele is a pure Ndwandwe because both his parents were Ndwandwe, a core group of the Ngoni, as well as a royal clan. In Ngoni to which he belongs were those who moved from Njuyu area to Mphongo near Mzimba Boma when the Livingstonia missionaries came into the area. This was after negotiations with Inkosi ya Makhosi M'mbelwa I at Ching'ambo near Kaning'ina in present day Mzuzu City. A true Ngoni is one who is born from parents that are of Ndwandwe origin from Zululand in South Africa. By all standards, no one can question his Ndwandwe descent. This group belonged to the Ngoni who settled in Malawi in the 1850s. The Ngoni are a nation of scores of ethnic groups who came together under the rule of Zwangendaba and M'mbelwa. The Ngoni name was coined after the crossing of the Zambezi for identity purposes. At this point in time there were so many tribes under the leadership of Zwangendaba who were fleeing the Mfecane wars as a result of the rise of Shaka Zulu.[18] Maintaining his culture, Jele married Hlupekile Nhlane, his cousin from a Swazi clan and daughter to his mother's brother, in 1952 the same month he started working.[19]

Unfortunately, Jele and his wife had no biological children but they kept children of their relatives. From the time Jele and his wife got married they have stayed faithful to one another until NyaNhlane was called to be with the Lord in 2011. This should be a lesson to some young ministers who do not have children to be faithful to one another and not to have children outside marriage.

---

[16] Interview Dr Jele, Etchiyeni village, Mphongo, 20.5.2009.

[17] Interview by telephone, Wyson Mkochi relative of Dr Jele, born to the sister of Nelly Nhlane, 13.8.2009.

[18] For the Ngoni migration see D.D. Phiri, *From Nguni to Ngoni*, Limbe: Popular Publications, 1982.

[19] Interview Dr Jele, Etchiyeni village, Mphongo, 20.5.2009.

Education

In 1939, Jele started his elementary school at Mphongo Village School, which is still known by the same name to the present day. This school is west of Mzimba Boma. After finishing elementary school, he went to do his standard one at Mzimba Full Primary School in 1942 and continued at that school until 1947.[20] In 1947 Jele transferred to Loudon-Chasefu mission station of CCAP Synod of Livingstonia where he continued his primary education until the time he wrote his standard six examinations in 1950.[21] By then Primary school was from Substandard A to Standard Six.

His stay at Loudon mission school brought him into contact with students from Zambia, especially those from Chasefu, who had come to study there. By then Loudon mission school was an international school, being open for students from Zambia and Malawi. Through this contact with Zambian students, Jele made friends with some of them who introduced him to life in Zambia, though it was not so distinct from Malawian life as they shared a great deal of values and norms. It is important to note that Loudon-Chasefu mission had two mission schools, one in Malawi, which was called Loudon Mission School, and another in Zambia, which was called Chasefu Mission School. Thus, political boundaries created by the Colonial Governments did not restrict people in Zambia and Malawi from living and working together. The contemporaries of Jele were free to work anywhere because of the education background. This could be the reason why later he did not find it difficult to work in Zambia.[22]

After passing his standard six government examinations in 1950, Jele went to the Roman Catholic secondary school in Zomba, often affectionately called "Box 2". Studying in Zomba made him develop some skills of leadership because of interaction with colleagues from all parts of Nyasaland. Further to this, Zomba was the capital of Nyasaland, drawing people, especially intellectuals, from all parts of Nyasaland. It is also said that some people came from Zambia and built houses in Zomba, and the area was named after a Zambian city, Ndola.[23] In Zomba Jele met many

---

[20] The school was run by Livingstonia Mission before it was handed over to the local education authority in the early 1960s.

[21] Interview Dr Jele, Etchiyeni village, Mphongo, 20.5.2009.

[22] Interview Dr Jele, Etchiyeni village, Mphongo, 20.5.2009.

[23] Told by Rev C. W. Mapala, whose grandfather, a Zambian by nationality, was part of the team building Ndola houses.

people from different parts of Malawi and Zambia. However, he failed to complete his senior secondary school and only went as far as Form II because of ill health. When he failed to complete his education, he immediately found a job with the colonial government, where he was employed as a veterinary clerk in Mzimba on 1 August 1952. This will be discussed in detail in chapter two.

CHAPTER TWO: WORK EXPERIENCE, CONVERSION AND CALL TO MINISTRY

Upon knowing Jele and discovering him, this chapter will now fully discuss Jele's work experience, his conversion which had led him to his call, his life at Theological College, ordination to the ministry and how he became a missionary in Zambia.

Work Experience as a Civil Servant

As mentioned in chapter two, Jele was employed as a veterinary clerk in Mzimba on 1 August 1952 by the Nyasaland Government, which tells us that he was a civil servant. In January 1953, he was transferred to Zomba Headquarters where he served from 1953 to 1954. Then in 1954, he was again transferred to Dedza District as District Veterinary Clerk. By then he was just a Christian in name only, which means that he had not yet received Jesus Christ as his personal Saviour, until 3 March 1959.[24] From Dedza Jele was again transferred back to Zomba in the same year 1954. In January 1960, he was transferred to Blantyre as a Provincial Officer on promotion from grade 'B' to grade 'A'. In all, he worked as a civil servant in the Nyasaland Government for ten years. This shows that his job as a veterinary clerk helped him to shape his leadership skills because he had an opportunity to meet different kinds of people from the lower class, middle class and higher class.

Conversion and Call into Holy Ministry

While working in Zomba, like any sons and daughters of Malawi, he and his colleagues were registered as freedom fighters with other civil servants to fight for the independence of Malawi.[25] It was in Zomba during the political unrest period between 1959 and 1962 while Jele was working as a civil servant in the colonial Government that Jele first professed openly his faith in Jesus Christ.

---

[24] Interview Dr Jele, Etchiyeni village, Mphongo, 20.5.2009.

[25] Interview Dr Jele, Etchiyeni village, Mphongo, 20.5.2009.

His conversion came between January and March 1959 during the time of political struggle led by Dr Hastings Kamuzu Banda who later became the first President of Malawi.[26] During this time, "people started destroying anything that belonged to Government, for example, bridges, roads, or posters were smashed and burnt. The civil servants organized what they called 'Civil Disobedience' and stayed in their homes and stopped going for work."[27] During the interviews, Jele described his thoughts and feelings on his conversion as follows:

On 3rd March 1959 in Zomba I first made my public confession that Jesus is my personal saviour. At one time people thought I was insane and they took me to the hospital after a demonstration during the political unrest. This conversion led me to my call to Holy ministry. This call was very dramatic because I didn't think of becoming a minister but it was what I professed in Jesus that made me to change my mind and think of joining the Holy ministry because I heard a small voice calling me for this ministry. My call was also more like Paul's vision (Acts 9:1-7) and after some time, I started preaching evangelistic messages. Then, in the same year 1959, I decided to apply for the Holy ministry under the Blantyre Synod. However, the church in Blantyre was reluctant to process my application. As a result, I was advised to apply through my home congregation in Milala Loudon-Chasefu Presbytery and I did. When God called me from government service to Holy ministry, it was very frightening, but God has not let me down. The fears Satan was putting before me have been proved groundless and futile. God is faithful; he has never let me to suffer.[28]

It was his dramatic call as witnessed above that made him to apply to study for holy ministry. We also see that what happened after his conversion made him to dedicate his life to work for the Lord and his motto was "With Jesus I will go anywhere He sends me."[29] This motto of Jele is significant for those modern Church Ministers who have different motives apart from serving the people they are called to serve. The motive should not be centred on self-service but on serving God and His people.

As indicated above, Jele responded to the call of God after his conversion during the years 1959 to 1962, when there was "political unrest

---

[26] Interview Dr Jele, Etchiyeni village, Mphongo, 20.5.2009. For a thorough study of the Emergency see: Kings Phiri, John McCracken, W.O. Mulwafu (eds), *Malawi in Crisis. The 1959/60 Nyasaland State of Emergency and its Legacy*, Zomba: Kachere, 2012.
[27] Interview Dr Jele, Etchiyeni village, Mphongo, 20.5.2009.
[28] Interview Dr Jele, Etchiyeni village, Mphongo, 20.5.2009.
[29] Interview Dr Jele, Etchiyeni village, Mphongo, 20.5.2009.

in Malawi, resulting in riots, deaths and civil disobedience."[30] The local people wanted independence from the colonial masters who had imposed on them against their wishes the Federation of Rhodesia and Nyasaland.[31] Jele also recalls that he was among the four men, who responded to the call to holy ministry of word and sacrament after the preaching of Jack Selfridge.[32] They became associates of Selfridge, a Scottish missionary, and Jele became a lifetime friend of Selfridge up to Selfridge's death. At one time "MCP political activists who hated everyone who accompanied white people" attacked them.[33] Jele reminisces what happened at that day:

> It was a Sunday when Jack Selfridge, my colleagues and I went to attend a Church service, when the thugs from the Malawi Congress Party (MCP) attacked us violently. We were almost killed but by the grace of God, we were saved when we prayed to God. As we were going home full of joy, we said to one another that we were almost killed today but we had no fear because the Lord we serve saved us. We had so much joy, that we could have died singing. We compared ourselves to the early apostles who had a similar situation and experience as it is recorded in Acts 5:40-41.[34] The other three friends were Franklin Chunga,[35] Richard Ndolo and Frank Ndhlazi who also became ministers of the word and sacraments in the CCAP Synod of Livingstonia.[36]

This experience also motivated Jele to respond faithfully to the call of our Lord and Saviour Jesus Christ to serve Him in difficult times as well as in

---

[30] Jack Selfridge, *Jack of all Trades Mastered by One*, p. 14

[31] Jack Selfridge, *Jack of all Trades Mastered by One*, p. 14

[32] Jack Selfridge was a faith missionary from Scotland and did most of his mission work in Malawi and Zambia who later became a very good friend of Wyson. For his autobiography see: Jack Selfridge, *Jack of All Trades Mastered by One,* Evanton, Scotland: Christian Focus Publications, 1996.

[33] Fergus McPherson, "The 1959 Emergency at Livingstonia" *in Bulletin of the Scottish Institute of Missionary Studies,* no. 10, 1994, p. 36.

[34] "They called the apostles in and had them flogged. Then they ordered them not to speak in the name of Jesus, and let them go. The apostles left the Sanhedrin, rejoicing because they had been counted worthy of suffering disgrace for the Name."

[35] See Victor Kaonga, "SCOM's founder the Reverend Franklin Chunga" http://ndagha.blogspot.com/2008/01/meet-rev-franklin-chunga-founder-of.html. For his work with SCOM see: Boston Khonje, The Establishment, Growth and Contribution of the Student Christian Organization of Malawi (SCOM) to the Malawian Society 1961-2012, MA, Mzuzu University, 2013.

[36] Interview Dr Jele, Etchiyeni village, Mphongo, 20.5.2009.

good times. In this incident, he might have died but his life was spared for a special purpose that has become a big testimony for him throughout his life. His conversion, as pointed out above, made him to apply for Holy ministry first in 1959 while working in Zomba as a Veterinary Clerk. After the Rev F.A. Chunga processed Jele's application at his home congregation, he resigned from Government service in November 1962 and went to his home in Mzimba from Blantyre. In the same month, November 1962, he went to visit his relatives on the Copperbelt of Zambia. In December 1962, he returned to Malawi in order to prepare for theological studies, which were to start in January 1963.[37] It seems he developed his interest to serve in Zambia at this period.

Life at Nkhoma Theological College

Jele went to Theological College at the time when Blantyre and Livingstonia Synods were joining to train ministers. The first joint groups were trained in Livingstonia Synod at Khondowe to enhance the Church unity. After some time, the Principal Charles Watt of the Joint College reported to the General Synod that the joint fellowship was working well. Then the General Synod resolved to include also Nkhoma and Harare Synods because by then the Synod of Zambia was not yet born. Harare became a Synod under Nkhoma Synod.[38] After the agreement, they decided to have one Theological College in Nkhoma. Therefore, Jele began his theological studies at Nkhoma Theological College in 1963, soon after the constitution of this college, which had joined all CCAP Synods together in by then Nyasaland (Malawi) and Southern Rhodesia (Zimbabwe).[39] This shows that Jele was among the first pioneer students of this Ecumenical College.

The students were drawn from Livingstonia, Blantyre, Nkhoma and Harare Synods. Some of the students from Livingstonia were the Very Rev Dr Silas M Nyirenda, (former Moderator of the General Assembly and the first Principal of Zomba Theological College which was opened in 1977),[40] Rev S.S. Lungu, retired and now stays in Loudon, Rev M.Z. Chavula retired who also served as chaplain at Ekwendeni Mission Hospital and the late Rev C.D. Sapao. From Blantyre came five students, Nkhoma sent one student by

---

[37] Interview Dr Jele, Etchiyeni village, Mphongo, 20.5.2009.
[38] Interview Dr Jele, Etchiyeni village, Mphongo, 20.5.2009.
[39] CCAP, General Synod minutes, no 4, 1964.
[40] He was also part of the team which was instrumental in establishing the College of Theology, University of Livingstonia at Ekwendeni which started as Livingstonia Theological College in 2003. Later he was the Chancellor of Livingstonia University.

the name of Rev Chalela, who is now in Lilongwe, and the late Rev Kalama who came from Harare Synod.[41] The duration of the course was three years and one-year probation. Jele graduated in 1965, receiving a Certificate in Theology, and he was ordained in 1967.

The life at this Ecumenical College (Nkhoma Theological College) shaped the life of young Jele as to what kind of a leader he would be. This ecumenical aspect made Jele not to have problems in serving people with different backgrounds, and this interaction helped him to develop the leadership skills he acquired.

Higher Education

Jele won a scholarship with the Emmanuel Bible School of Theology, Birkenhead in the Liverpool area, Cheshire. In 1967, he left Malawi for Great Britain to pursue a Diploma in Theology at Emmanuel Bible College for two years. While studying at this college, Jele's wife, Sylvia Nhlane, was also doing her studies in English Grammar and Biblical Instruction at Emmanuel Bible School.[42] It was also during this period that the International Free Protestant Episcopal University, London, honoured Jele with the degree of "Doctor of Theology", certificate no. 1617 of June 1968. Jele gave the details:

> This award was a proposal by the London Theologians to award me with an Honorary Degree of Doctor of Theology. The suggestions came from Doctors who had heard me preaching in some of their churches where I used to preach during holidays. Thereafter I was questioned by the Doctors of Theology in London where I took my training and what subjects in Church Ministry I took, what I was studying by then and my personal testimony of Jesus as Saviour and Lord. From these experiences, they found it necessary to award me the Honorary Degree of Doctor of Theology. This award had nothing to do with the college where I was doing studies. However, upon completion from Emmanuel Bible College I received the Diploma in Theology and Missionary Certificate.[43]

---

[41] Interview Dr Jele, Etchiyeni village, Mphongo, 20.5.2009.

[42] Interview Dr Jele, Etchiyeni village, Mphongo, 20.5.2009.

[43] Interview Dr Jele, Etchiyeni village, Mphongo, 20.5.2009.

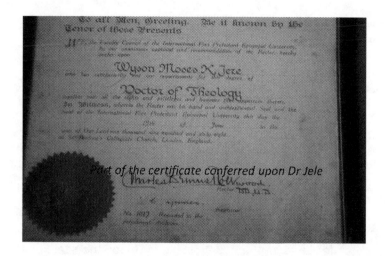
Part of the certificate conferred upon Dr Jele

What is interesting in his statement is that the people who awarded him a doctoral degree inquired of his former theological training. Thus, it appears that no one in Great Britain anticipated an African pastor could have acquired such skill in preaching. Therefore, Jele's studies and the interactions he had, enhanced his understanding of mission work. It was his zeal on preaching that led to the award of his Doctorate Degree. Therefore,

Jele with Rev Chavula

he is called Rev Dr Wyson Moses Kauzobafa Jele. All he received was in preparation for what he was to become and continued to be. While still in Britain, Jele heard of a programme known as "New Life For All" and became interested in this programme until it came to Malawi. He returned from Britain to Malawi in August 1969. When this programme came to Malawi, from 1973 to 1981 he served as National Chairperson of this para-church organization,[44] which played a major role in the Blantyre Spiritual Awakening.[45]

Ordination to the Holy Ministry and Experience in the Church

At this moment it is important to explore his life and training. Jele graduated from Nkhoma Theological College in 1965. After completing his studies at Nkhoma Theological College, he was allocated to Elangeni congregation of Loudon-Chasefu Presbytery in 1966.[46] After serving there for a year, he was ordained in January 1967 at Mabili Congregation at the time Rev Patrick Ng'anjo was both Synod Moderator and Moderator for Loudon-Chasefu Presbytery. It was the same year that Jele left for further studies at Emmanuel Bible College in Great Britain.[47]

After ordination in 1967 Jele did not only serve in various congregations but also received appointments to serve in different capacities. For instance, upon graduating from Emmanuel Bible College in 1969, he returned home in August. In 1970, he was elected Moderator of Loudon-Chasefu Presbytery. This was a preparation to serve in Zambia because as Moderator he also used to travel to Chasefu and see how the church was doing there.[48] In 1971, he was transferred to Milala Congregation in Mzimba. Then in 1976 Dr Jele and Rev Ndolo were appointed to revise the *Ndondomeko ya Visopo* (Order of Service) for use in the Synod of Livingstonia congregations. This same *Ndondomeko ya Visopo* is also used in the CCAP Synod of Zambia congregations. Then, from 1977 August to 1980 September, he served as Head of Station at Lwasozi Congregation in Loudon Mission. In 1979/1980, Jele was elected as Moderator for the Synod of Livingstonia and became spiritual pastor for Synod of Livingstonia

---

[44] Interview Dr Jele, Etchiyeni village, Mphongo, 20.5.2009.

[45] For details see: Bright Kawamba, The Blantyre Spiritual Awakening 1969 to 1986: An Antecedent of the Charismatic Movement in Malawi, MA, University of Malawi, 2013.

[46] For Livingstonia Synod of those years see: Moses Mlenga, "Fifty Years of Post-Missionary Leadership in Livingstonia Synod, 1958 to 2008," Mzuni Documents 251, Mzuzu: Mzuni Press, 2009.

[47] Interview Dr Jele, Etchiyeni village, Mphongo, 20.5.2009.

[48] Interview Dr Jele, Etchiyeni village, Mphongo, 20.5.2009.

congregations and Zambian congregations. After retiring from this position, he was appointed as the first full time Evangelism Secretary in 1980.[49]

In his career as a minister of the word and sacraments, he has been honoured with several certificates of recognition from General Synod, Synod of Livingstonia and his Presbytery, conferences and workshops. For example, the Haggai Institute for Advanced Leadership Training awarded Jele a Certificate of Attendance in Christian Leadership after successfully completing the specialized studies in Christian Leadership; Milala Presbytery awarded Jele the certificate of appreciation of good service, for having served the Presbytery after retirement from 1997 to 2004 when the Presbytery had a serious shortage of Ministers. The General Synod honoured him with a Certificate of Special Recognition in memory of Mission Work of the Scottish Church in Malawi for 125 years in August 2000 as can be seen below. Loudon Presbytery had honoured him with several certificates because of the services he had rendered in their Presbytery as can be seen below: [50]

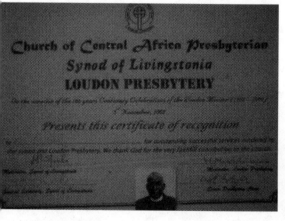

Certificates of Recognition

[49] Interview Dr Jele, Mzuzu, 3.9.2009.

[50] Interview Dr Jele, Etchiyeni village, Mphongo, 20.5.2009.

Apart from serving in the CCAP Synod of Livingstonia, Jele also served as National Chairperson of New Life For All in Malawi,[51] as an Executive Board Member of the Evangelical Fellowship of Malawi (EFM), which was a member body of the Evangelical Fellowship of Africa and Madagascar, led by Dr Byang Kato. This EFM was affiliated to the World Evangelical Fellowship (WEF). Furthermore, Jele attended several world conferences such as; Evangelism Tour and Conferences in Birmingham England 1974, Pan Africa Leadership Conference in 1976 in Nairobi Kenya, Extensive Evangelism Conference "Love Africa" in Blantyre Malawi 1978, General Assembly of the Church of Scotland and Northern Ireland 1979, Extensive Evangelism Course and Conference in Singapore 1981, World Evangelism Conference, Amsterdam, Netherlands in 1983.[52]

Becoming a Missionary in Zambia

Just like any other Malawian minister who had served in Zambia, Jele was also appointed as a local missionary in November 1981. He took over from Rev Chaula, who was a minister at Matero congregation. This is how he recalled his early days as a missionary:

> There was a time when a need arose in Zambia for senior ministers to help the Church in Lusaka and the Copperbelt. I was appointed a local missionary together with Rev J.W. Kamanga. I went straight to Lusaka and Rev Kamanga went to Kitwe. The Church in Zambia started growing fast despite the problems we encountered. At that time, we were under Chasefu Presbytery, but in November 1982 Lusaka/Copperbelt Presbytery was born and I was the first Moderator of the new Presbytery, while Rev Newstead Mtonga was the first Presbytery clerk. At this time the congregations were Lusaka, Ndola, Wusakile, Kalulushi, Mufulira, Chingola and Chililabombwe.[53]

---

[51] For the crucial role of New Life For All in the Blantyre Awakening see: Bright Kawamba, The Blantyre Spiritual Awakening 1969 to 1986: An Antecedent of the Charismatic Movement in Malawi, MA, University of Malawi, 2013.

[52] Interview Dr Jele, Etchiyeni village, Mphongo, 20.5.2009. For the conference records see: www2.wheaton.edu/bgc/archives/guides/253.htm.

[53] Interview Dr Jele, Etchiyeni village, Mphongo, 20.5.2009.

From this appointment, Jele and his colleagues worked very hard and by 1984, the work in Zambia had grown to a reasonable size, age and shape. Then the General Synod of the CCAP and the Synod of Livingstonia considered the Church in Zambia to be a Synod of its own. In order to do this, a caretaker committee was formed in 1983 and Jele was the chairperson of this caretaker committee. Other members were Rev F.Y. Ndhlazi as secretary, while members were Rev S.M. Mithi, Rev N.M. Mtonga, Mr L.V. Zimba, Mr F.N. Chilembo (late) and Mr J.D. Mtonga (late). On 8th June 1983, the caretaker committee met and resolved that for now the Synod Headquarters should be at Lundazi, but that in the future, once the Synod is financially stable, the offices would be moved to Lusaka.[54] (The Synod office was moved to Lusaka in 1995 by then the General Secretary, Rev D. Chiboboka, who is now Principal of Chasefu Theological College.) When all was ready and after all the arrangements were made, Jele was transferred from Lusaka to Lundazi on 1 October 1984.[55]

From 26th to 28th October, 1984 the General Synod met in Lundazi and on 28 October, 1984 the CCAP Synod of Zambia was inaugurated. The inauguration of the CCAP Synod of Zambia was a great day because members of the General Synod CCAP were well represented. Fifty delegates witnessed the inauguration of the Synod of Zambia at Lundazi in the Eastern Province of Zambia. Further, this ceremony was witnessed by a great gathering of about 4,000 people from all over Zambia.[56] Among those who witnessed this great occasion were government representatives like Hon F.C.M. Nyirongo, the then Governor of Lundazi and acting Governor of Chama, Chiefs Magodi IV of Lundazi, Chibale of Chama, Muyombe of Isoka District, Rev R.N. Daka of the Reformed Church in Zambia (RCZ) and delegates from the Roman Catholic Church.[57]

After the inauguration of the CCAP Synod of Zambia, on 27 October 1984, the following were elected to run this newly constituted Church:

Moderator, Rev S.M. Mithi (Zambian),
Moderator Elect, Rev N.M. Mtonga (Zambian),
General Secretary, Rev Dr W.M.K. Jele (Malawian),
Deputy General Secretary, Rev F.J. Mwanza (Zambian)

---

[54] Interview Dr Jele, Etchiyeni village, Mphongo, 20.5.2009.
[55] Minutes of Synod meeting of CCAP Synod of Zambia, 1984.
[56] Minutes of Synod meeting of CCAP Synod of Zambia, 1984.
[57] Minutes of Synod meeting of CCAP Synod of Zambia, 1984.

General Treasurer, Mr Lameck V. Zimba (Zambian),

Executive members: Mr F.N. Chirambo, Mr Nickson Ngulube, and Mr J.T. Kamanga, all Zambians, and Mr Jairos S. Lungu, a Malawian.

Umanyano workers were: Mama Catherine Mazunda – Synod worker,

Mama Ethel NyaMtonga – Presbytery worker.[58]

When the Synod was constituted in 1984, the CCAP church in Zambia had only four indigenous ordained ministers; these were Rev S.M. Mithi, Rev N.M. Mtonga, Rev F.J. Mwanza and Rev T.K.M. Zyambo.[59] Besides the four ordained ministers there were also four Presbytery evangelists. These were: Messrs Harry C. Nyirenda, Edward Tom Moyo, Tyford J. Mithi and Morris J. Simwaba. The Synod of Livingstonia had left only two Malawian ministers to assist in Zambia, Rev Dr W.M.K. Jele and Rev F.Y. Ndhlazi.[60] The congregations were only 10, while Presbyteries were only two: Chasefu and Midlands/Copperbelt, and communicants were fewer than 10,000.[61] However, when this study was carried out, the following were the current statistics as of 30th August, 2013:

Presbyteries had risen to 12, and Ministers to 72. 9 Student Ministers, two are at Justo Mwale Theological University College, 6 are at Chasefu, (now the Synod has an American missionary by the name of Rev Kari Joy Nicewander who is working as Mission and Evangelism Specialist), Chasefu Theological College (Offers a diploma Programme which Theological College and one is at College of Theology, University of Livingstonia. Communicants were 63,432, Congregations 74, Prayer houses 235, Mission Schools 14 and Community Schools 14. Clinics two. Besides the necessary Departments, the Synod has Women's Guild, Men's Guild and Christian Youth Fellowship (CYF), Education, Health, Shallow Wells, Relief and Development, HIV/AIDS, Literature, Lay Training, Mission and Evangelism is affiliated to the University of Livingstonia in

---

[58] Victor Chilenje, PhD Thesis, p. 196.

[59] Out of these four only Rev S. M. Mithi and Rev N.M. Mtonga are still serving while Rev T.K.M. Zyambo was deposed in 1986 and Rev F. J. Mwanza passed on in 2006.

[60] Victor Chilenje, PhD Thesis, p. 194.

[61] Minutes of Synod meeting of CCAP Synod of Zambia, 1984.

Malawi), Media Department (the Synod has employed a media specialist, an American missionary by the name of Joe Dejong), Project and Development Department (PDD).

These statistics show that the CCAP Synod of Zambia has grown much compared to the time Jele was its leader. The Church has close relations with the Reformed Church in Zambia (RCZ), the United Church of Zambia (UCZ) and the Uniting Presbyterian Church of Zambia (UPCSA). The church is also a member of the Council of Churches in Zambia (CCZ), of Theological Education by Extension in Zambia (TEEZ), Bible Society of Zambia (BSZ), Reformed Ecumenical Council (REC), and Evangelical Fellowship in Zambia (EFZ) and Council of Reformed Churches in Southern Africa (CRCSA).[62] The CCAP Synod of Zambia carries on a missionary witness by having organized preaching stations (prayer houses) and local evangelists at both congregational level and Presbytery level. The CCAP Synod of Zambia also organizes evangelism out-reach campaigns with the help of the men's guild, the women's guild and the youth who are known as the Christian Youth Fellowship (CYF). However, even though it was given its independent status, CCAP Synod of Livingstonia still sends missionaries to Zambia when need arises.[63]

Jele served in Zambia for seven years from November 1981 to November 1988, before returning to Malawi. Even though Jele returned to Malawi, the CCAP Synod of Zambia has extended their invitation to him to attend the Synod meetings as a life member. After returning to Malawi, he was allocated to Mzuzu Congregation and by then almost all the congregations in Mzuzu were under Mzuzu congregation. After serving for some time in Mzuzu, Jele asked the Synod to send him to a nearby congregation because he was about to retire, so the Synod of Livingstonia sent him to Kamilaza in 1989. He served at Kamilaza up to 1994. In 1994, Jele officially retired. After retirement, he worked with the Evangelical Association of Malawi (EAM) as an Executive Board member. As per Synod of Livingstonia policy, after retirement the Church minister is free to work with it on contract basis. Thus, after seeing the gifts and potential Jele had, the Synod, through Milala Presbytery, asked Jele to help by serving at

---

[62] Victor Chilenje, *The Origin and Development of the Church of Central Africa Presbyterian in Zambia 1882-2004,* PhD, Stellenbosch University, p. iv.
[63] Interview Dr Jele, Etchiyeni village, Mphongo, Mzimba, 20.5.2009.

Katolonji, one of the congregations in Milala Presbytery.[64] Finally Jele ended his full-time ministry in 2005.

---

[64] Interview Dr Jele, Etchiyeni village, Mphongo, Mzimba, 3.9.2009.

CHAPTER THREE: HIS WORK IN CCAP SYNOD OF ZAMBIA

This chapter will look at Jele's work in the newly inaugurated CCAP Synod of Zambia, by re-examining his leadership, his impact or contribution to the church, as a Parish Minister, Administrator, and lastly his legacy to the CCAP Synod of Zambia. Before looking at his work I will first define what Leadership is.

Definition of Leadership

Rick Joyner defines leadership as "the ability to mobilize others to accomplish a common goal."[65] In addition, he says that "successful leadership is vision combined with ability to resolve, encourage, and endurance that takes one to accomplish the goal, to press the job until it is finished."[66] To add to this, Kouzes and Posner believe that "leadership is ultimately about creating a way for people to contribute to something extraordinary to happen."[67]

The definitions above perfectly describe the leadership of Jele who demonstrated the ability to motivate the members of CCAP Synod of Zambia to participate in the building of the church to what it is today. His going there, as a senior minister, was to spearhead the Zambian leaders to engage with conflict resolution on the problems the church encountered in Lusaka and Copperbelt provinces. Hence, I will contend that it was his good skills, which reconciled the CCAP members in Lusaka and Copperbelt to work together as a family;[68] possibly, he was effective because of his ecumenical background.

---

[65] Rick Joyner, *Leadership the Power of a Creative Life*, Fort Mill: Morningstar Publications, 2007, p. 12.
[66] Rick Joyner, p. 12.
[67] Barry Z. Kouzes and James M. Posner, *Leadership Challenge,* p. 3.
[68] Interview Mr. B.K. Mbewe, Matero, 9.7.2009.

Jele as an Outstanding Leader in Zambia

A cross section of the members of the Synod of Zambia interviewed described Jele as an exceptional and innovative leader. Some of the virtues of Jele were decency, courage, and industriousness. He was a principled, broadminded leader and one able to give sound advice. He believed in collaborative and participatory ministry. He was a church planter who knew his duties and was an influential leader who was firm and inspiring and knew where he wanted to take the Church to. This could be the reason why Rev Dr Victor Chilenje[69] and Rev S.M. Mithi[70] describe him as a visionary and composed leader, who had the heart of developing the Church in Zambia for God's glory.[71] The description demonstrates the kind of leader Jele was as one who defined the goals and gathered the necessary resources in order to train others to accomplish the goals. In all he refused to let obstacles stop him or divert him from his course. Further, he also showed servanthood by being humble, willing to serve and not to be served. In other words, Jele's leadership can be compared to Nehemiah the builder (Nehemiah 1:1-11) and to a pastor like Timothy (2 Timothy 1:1-7). Like Nehemiah, Jele was a man of prayer and he made prayer an ordinary part of living and working.[72] He was decisive in leading; he had ability to organize, was brave in face of opposition, persevered and was always setting right priorities for God's work.

Jele as Administrator and Evangelist in Zambia

J ele was not only an outstanding leader, he was also an administrator and evangelist. He had unique leadership skills in both his administrative and evangelistic approach. The uniqueness of Jele's leadership was that he was a leader who believed in the word of God and regarded the word as the center of his call. Even though others can argue that all leaders believe

---

[69]   Rev Dr Victor Chilenje was one of the ministers that Dr Jele groomed. He once served as the General Secretary of the CCAP Synod of Zambia. The time this study was carried out he was the Moderator-Elect.

[70]   Rev Substone Mithi was the first Zambian minister to work with Dr Jele and was the first Synod Moderator for CCAP Synod of Zambia.

[71]   Interviews Rev Dr Chilenje and Rev S.M. Mithi.

[72]   Oswald Sanders, *Spiritual Leadership: Principles of Excellence for Every Believer,* Chicago: Moody Press, 1994, p. 163.

in the word of God, his zeal for the word is unique. His uniqueness was that he was able to bring his flock to the right teaching. As pointed out above, he was brave in the face of opposition, was an industrious and visionary leader and was a leader who was determined to deal with administrative issues as they come to him. This could be the reason why Dr Chilenje says, "some leaders are non-starters, but Jele did not bother to take risks wherever it was necessary to do so."[73] This means that he was serious with whatever he was doing and could not mind the consequences. It can be safely said that a true leader is one who is principled, and determined to take risks if need arises. Thus, Jele was one of such leader.

What made Jele's leadership unique is the aspect of delegation, he did not do most of his work alone but he delegated some of his duties to other people to enable them to learn leadership skills. He believed in *"zosiyilana"* philosophy. (To encourage others to take responsibilities even though a leader is not present). For instance, Prophet Elijah trained Elisha with the intention that Elisha would take over from him in his absence. Jele did the same. Further, Mr. Chima of Lundazi, who served as his session clerk, said that Dr Jele was the kind of leader who really wanted to develop others not only spiritually, but also physically, mentally, emotionally and economically by making the members to be self-supporting.[74] This can be seen through the work he did at Lundazi. He built a house for a carpentry shop so that some members could be employed there, be trained there, and generate income for the church.

Such continuity is an essential component of any institution's sustainability. If capacity building is not part of the vision of the church then its future is ambiguous. This could be the reason why Jack Thompson in his article "African Leadership in Livingstonia Mission 1875-1900" quoted Robert Laws who argued that, "if Africa is to be won for Christ there are no two ways about it—it will be won by the Africans themselves."[75] The change and progress was so quick and fruitful because Jele was not only African but he was well placed to understand the Zambian worldview.

---

[73] Interview Dr Chilenje, Lundazi, 19.7.2009.
[74] Interview Mr Chima, Lundazi, 20.7.2009.
[75] T.J. Thompson, *African Leadership in Livingstonia Mission 1875-1900,* in *Journal of Social Science*, Vol. II, 1973, p. 81.

Life in the Parish in Zambia

In Zambia Jele served as a Parish Minister in Lusaka at Matero congregation and in Lundazi at Lundazi North congregation.

In November 1981, Jele was appointed minister in charge of Matero Congregation in George Compound, because by then it was the only prayer house, which had a church building. While stationed in Matero Jele managed to visit other prayer points in Lusaka.[76] Although he succeeded in establishing the church in Lusaka, he encountered a number of challenges. The first was the problem of accommodation as there were no manses and no places of worship. At times, they used to worship in classroom blocks or under trees.

Despite encountering these challenges in these prayer points, he is described as an exceptional pastor, who knew how to tend his flock, caring, feeding, guiding, protecting and comforting them. He was a pastor who liked prayers and often he used to set days for prayer and fasting where people would come and be prayed for and at the same time pray for their needs. However, many pastors describe this as charismatic, but Jele knew that a prayer could heal and change a life. Rev Kondwani Nkhoma, the first female minister in the CCAP Synod of Zambia, says, "it was Jele who first prayed for me to know Jesus Christ as my personal Saviour."[77] She also pointed out that, "it was Jele who introduced morning prayers at Lundazi Boma Prayer House, now David MacConaghy Congregation."[78] These morning prayers initiated by him are still continuing at David MacConaghy congregation in Lundazi Boma.

On 1 October 1984, Jele was transferred to Lundazi so that he and other colleagues could speed up the process of making Zambia CCAP an autonomous Synod.

As pointed out already, Jele believed that delegation is one of the ways that a leader can use, only if those to be delegated are well equipped through training. Therefore, as a pastor in a congregation, he was good at training elders and deacons. This shows that he was a leader who was willing to develop others to continue the work of the Lord. As a leader, he taught his elders and deacons to understand the Church government of CCAP. Jele also taught the members how to face realities in life and how to obey God's word and how to dialogue with others. In so doing, Jele

---

[76] Interview B.K. Mbewe. Matero, Lusaka, 9.7.2009.
[77] Interview Rev K. Nkhoma, Mandevu, Lusaka, 13.7.2009.
[78] Interview Rev K. Nkhoma, Mandevu, Lusaka, 13.7.2009.

encouraged the members to live a life of prayer and pray with one another just like the early Christians did in Acts 2:42-47 which stands as a hallmark of what believers everywhere should seek to be in the church. Further, he also encouraged people to repent of their wrong doings by losing their face and their ego, that is to confess their sins by completely surrendering to Christ as their personal Saviour. This also echoes Acts 2:37-41 where Peter preached and thereafter people repented and received baptism. This enabled them to regain a new corporate identity by experiencing the love of God, acceptance and forgiveness.

As a result of his leadership skills as a pastor, the Church in Lusaka grew rapidly in numbers. Like in doing a puzzle, one need to have the right original for the pieces, otherwise the final product, the picture, turns out wrong, and the individual pieces do not make sense. This is what had happened in Lusaka, the right pieces who were the members were fitted wrongly because of fear, tradition, religious jealousy and a power and control mentality. However, Jele managed to put things in order through his teaching and his "good public relations and ecumenical mind, relation to parishioners, fellow Church ministers within and outside CCAP as well as the community at large."[79] Thus, Jele developed a favourable environment for all believers in Christ in Lusaka.

His ecumenical background enabled him to solve some pertinent issues in Zambia, in respect to those who broke away from the Reformed Church in Zambia (RCZ). The way he handled the issue surprised both the members within CCAP and those from different denominations. In the end, he earned himself respect, especially from those ministers who were against those who broke away from their churches, and he was described as a leader with a strong character and as fearless because of his courage.[80] As a Parish Minister, he also played a big role in establishing the men's and women's guilds and Christian Youth Fellowship (CYF) in Lusaka and other parts of the Midlands/Copperbelt Presbytery. Thus, Jele as a pastor differs from the shepherds Ezekiel describes in his prophecy; the ones who do not feed the sheep, but only want to exploit, who are not caring but rule harshly and who do not want to seek but to scatter (Ezekiel 34:1-10). Jele's passion and zeal was to serve the sheep and not his own glory.

---

[79] Interview Mr B.K. Mbewe, Matero, *Lusaka*, 9.7.2009.

[80] Interview Mr Mtambo, Chilenje, Lusaka, 14.7.2009.

A man knocking on the doors of his flock

Jele ready to go and preach the gospel

Pastoral ministry requires enough time for supervision and distinctive administrative skills in executing the institutional procedures. Based on the principle of "follow-your-leader," Jele was at the forefront in demonstrating the Christian life. He had the desire to worship God so that his members could have the same desire as well. He was good in preaching and teaching and always cheerful in his dealings, and his heart was always on winning souls for Christ. Therefore, in pastoral visitation he was trying to bring the church to the people by visiting them and not only to bring people to the church. In doing so he knew that the mission of the church was being accomplished and that it could only be accomplished by visiting the parishioners and finding out from them how they could be helped. It is said that he never got tired of visiting, even though in Lusaka there were many congregations, which he had planted, but he managed to visit all the congregations almost every week.[81] It was the same in Lundazi because it is confirmed that Jele used to visit his parishioners regularly, even though he was full time General Secretary.

During pastoral visitation, he encouraged members to have Bible study because that is how their faith could grow and if he found something strange or a problem he would get some elders to go with him another day so that he could solve that problem. Jele was not visiting people so that he could get some food at the end of the day, but he devoted much of his time to this work so that he could help those who had no time to come to Church. In support of this argument Rolina Ngwira says that "when he visited parishioners, he was always encouraging people to come to church and hear the word of God which gives life through our Lord Jesus Christ."[82]

---

[81] Interview Mr Mtambo, Chilenje, Lusaka, 14.7.2009.

[82] Interview Rolina Ngwira, Lundazi, 19.7.2009.

He did door to door pastoral visitation to encourage the people in their faith, and this also helped him to know each parishioner.

Jele and the Gospel: Prayer Warrior or Evangelist

We will begin this section by defining evangelism. Bryan Green defines evangelism as "preaching the Gospel".[83] The Collins English dictionary defines evangelism as the practice of spreading the Christian Gospel. This Gospel is the life, work, teachings, healings, death, resurrection and ascension of our Lord Jesus Christ. Evangelism should be holistic. Basing his work on this understanding Jele believed that his evangelistic style could be geared to bring the lost souls to Christ. Mr James Chidundu Ngwata says that his messages were of an evangelistic type because his aim was to win souls for Christ's kingdom. Though not underestimating the role of numbers, evangelism should be geared for qualitative discipleship. Categorically it can be said that Jele's evangelistic approach and messages were effective, because he used to spend time to know the people to whom he was ministering. It is paramount for every leader to get to know the needs of the people to whom one is ministering. It is the knowledge of the people that includes their history, their customs, and their beliefs that matter most in effective evangelism.

Effective evangelism can only be realized if the culture, language, customs and background of the people are understood.[84] This might explain why his preaching was relevant to the people because he used contemporary illustrations from the context of the people among whom he lived. He valued contextualization as the best tool to reach out to a person. He followed the example of Jesus who used parables in preaching and teaching. In these parables, Jesus spoke of things that were common to the people.[85] Jele also used metaphors that people understood well for effective response. Therefore, he made an impact on the people he evangelized because he understood their historical background. In his evangelism, he employed the methods of preaching, teaching, personal contact and instruction as stipulated in CCAP teaching. People who were to be baptized had to attend classes before baptism. This is the reason I argue

---

[83] Bryan Green, *The Practice of Evangelism*, London: Hodder and Stoughton, 1958, p. 15

[84] Interview Rev S.M. Mithi, Kanyama, Lusaka, 14.7.2009.

[85] Interview Mr Ngwata, Kanyama, Lusaka, 15.7.2009.

that teaching before baptism sets up a good background for the future Church to grow demographically and spiritually.

Rev Chilenje likens Jele's preaching to that of John the Baptist, who preached a message of repentance. He went on to say that when Jele preached his sermons they were like an axe that was ready to cut because most people responded positively to the message.[86] This shows that Jele' sermons were based on repentance and confession of one's sins. However, it is not that his preaching was only on repentance and confession, but it was his main thrust.

In his evangelistic messages, he also emphasized church planting. He followed the pattern of the early apostles as recorded in the book of Acts, which contains evidence of early steps taken to establish Churches among the people who had accepted their messages (Acts 14-19). This may be the reason why we see that even though Jele was based in Matero, he managed to supervise prayer points in Chilenje, Kayama, Mtendere and other parts of Lusaka. He used to organize evangelism rallies in these areas and could go on Wednesday to one place to do evangelism and Thursday and Friday conduct baptismal lessons and Saturday baptism. In this way, the church in Lusaka grew very fast. The people who were evangelized by Jele during his time are strong members in Lusaka. For instance, Mr Thompson Mtambo and Mr James Ngwata recall that Jele was able in each week to visit the various church *locations*[87] he had evangelized by holding prayers whether in houses or under trees. This approach made many people join the CCAP.[88] When he was in Lundazi as a Parish Minister, he used the same strategy he used in Lusaka.

In Lundazi, Chipata and Chama he went on further to form evangelism zones because by then it was called Chasefu Presbytery and it was very big.[89] This division was the preparation for what we now see as Presbyteries. Chasefu Presbytery has been divided into the following presbyteries; Chasefu, Lundazi East, Lundazi West, Haliday, Lumezi, Chipata and Northern. These divisions show that the church in Zambia is growing. For this reason, Dr Chilenje said,

---

[86] Interview Rev Dr V Chilenje, Lundazi, 19.7.2009.

[87] Location refers to designated areas within a township or district where people live.

[88] Interview Mr. Mtambo, Chilenje 14.7.2009 and Mr. Ngwata, Kayama, Lusaka, 15.7.2009.

[89] Interview Rev Dr Victor Chilenje, Lundazi, 19.7.2009.

Even though he was full time General Secretary he still spared some time to do evangelism and during his time they used to have many evangelism rallies and at times he used to invite evangelists from Malawi to come and preach and plant churches.[90]

Therefore, evangelism serves to nurture the life of the converted members, to evangelize people within the locality and to promote the kingdom of God, as it were, in the world.

Jele as General Secretary

As pointed out above, Jele was elected General Secretary on 27 October 1984, and was given Lundazi North congregation because of a shortage of ministers. The CCAP Synod of Zambia started without anything apart from a gift of a few Tumbuka and Chewa Hymn books donated by the General Synod.[91] While Jele's election into office was because of the leadership qualities discussed above, additionally, a lot of elders have said that he was elected into this office because he was the most educated by then, he had better qualifications and people had no doubt that he could run the Church well. He was a dignified and respected person who used diplomacy in his approaches. However, we could add that he was elected not only because of his leadership qualities, but also because of his vast experience in the Synod of Livingstonia as a Synod Moderator and Evangelism Secretary. His exposure and educational background gave confidence to the people that he could lead the Church. Above all, the way he had handled the conflicts in Matero and Ndola with the Reformed Church in Zambia and the Presbyterian Church in Zambia (PCZ), recommended him to be elected to the office of the General Secretary.

His Administration and Challenges

Jele's administration was exceptional because of the manner in which he handled administrative issues in the Synod. This could be because of the background experience he had acquired through the positions he had held before he came to Zambia. Jele, like Sangaya, also faced many problems

---

90 Interview Rev Dr Victor Chilenje, Lundazi, 19.7.2009.

91 Minutes of Synod Meeting of CCAP Synod of Zambia, 1984.

when he took over as the first General Secretary. Firstly, there was the acute shortage of ordained Zambian ministers;[92] secondly, that he was the first person to take up the job was a challenge in itself because he had no one to look to for guidance. Thirdly, there was the problem of finances. The new church had no finances to support its work. Lastly, he faced the problem of infrastructure like church buildings and manses for ministers, both those serving and those coming from College. As well, he faced the problem of transport, which made some ministers to walk on foot because by then it was difficult to buy a bicycle.[93]

Jele at a funeral

Even though he had these challenges, his administrative style made CCAP in Zambia to grow fast demographically and structurally. Demographic refers to numerical increase in Church members. Structural refers to capacity building and development infrastructure. His administration aimed at developing others and exposing the church to partners who came on board to help in building this new Synod. Jele tried to encourage young men to apply for holy ministry so that the church could be spread to all provinces in Zambia. Nevertheless, it was difficult, because most of them wanted white-collar jobs and to work in the mines of the Copperbelt where they could receive a lot of money rather than in the holy

---

[92] Silas S. Ncozana, p. 35.

[93] Interview Dr Victor Chilenje, 19.12.2009.

ministry.[94] He prepared his parishioners by sharing his visions, outlined the steps towards fulfilling the vision, prepared and organized resources and materials appropriate for each task, and he also built a close relationship with members of his team (I Chronicles 28:11-19). He was a leader who could implement, monitor and evaluate just as Nehemiah did. He was decisive in implementing what was agreed by the church through delegation or by him. He was a leader who kept time and did not want to delay in dealing with difficult people or situations.[95]

Jele as a Development Innovator and Initiator

Jele was not only punctual, he was also innovative and initiative. He initiated a great deal of projects. For instance, while he was General Secretary he initiated developmental activities in the Church. As projects require many resources, he developed a good network with overseas Presbyterian churches. He exposed the newly constituted Synod to overseas partners in the United Kingdom and in the United States of America. These partners assisted in building the church in the area of projects. These partners were the Presbyterian Church in Ireland (PCI) and the Presbyterian Church of the United States of America, PC(USA).[96] This exposure has made the church in Zambia to have additional partners such as the Presbyterian Church of Australia (PCA). These partners have assisted the Synod of Zambia financially and morally.

It was his initiative and creativity that enabled him to source the money to fence the former Synod headquarters' premises in Lundazi Boma, currently known as the David MacConaghy Lay Training Center. This project is not only historical but also interesting. It is interesting in the sense that some members thought that he was just wasting the money, but now they are appreciating him for the work he did because that place is now secured and no one can erect any building within the Church premises. In most places where the CCAP Synod Churches had big lands, the church has lost a lot of land by not protecting it in the way he did. For instance, in Chama the church has lost the land and now they are told to pay for the land, which was theirs; also in Lusaka in places like Mandevu, Chawama and Chilenje the church has lost much of the land, just because they did not protect it by fencing. This tells us that as leaders we have to make sure that we preserve

---

[94]   Interview Dr Jele, Etchiyeni village, Mphongo, 20.5.2009.

[95]   Interview Mr. B.K. Mbewe, *Matero*, 9.7.2009

[96]   Interview Rev Dr Victor Chilenje, Lundazi, 19.7.2009.

the land we are given by putting up some structures so that the lands of the church are protected and that it is on title deed. Although building fences is the best way of preserving the land, there are other equally good ways such as land lease and putting land on title deeds. However, in the absence of land lease fencing was the best option.

Effective running of the Church requires effective and reliable transport. This might be the reason Jele sourced money to purchase a Land Rover for the Church. It was procured for evangelism because previously they were only using bicycles for evangelism. In 1985, the Presbyterian Church of the United States of America donated a Land Rover; this was the first vehicle the church acquired.[97] The second vehicle was bought in 1999 after about fourteen years and about eleven years after Jele had gone back to Malawi. The number of vehicles now has risen to about thirteen, including the first Land Rover, even though now it is not working as it used to work.[98]

As General Secretary, he also managed to secure the necessary office equipment. He wrote to the CCAP Synod of Livingstonia to assist the newly constituted Synod with typewriters and his request was accepted. A typewriter and duplicator were donated and then the General Secretary of Synod of Livingstonia bought a second-hand typewriter from a donation from students in America under the auspices of the Rev Augustine M. Mfune. The Presbyterian Church in Ireland (PCI) donated an Off-Set Printing Machine. This machine was for the printing of hymns, church bulletins and other materials for the church, which is not working at the present day. The contacts Jele established were not to benefit him, but they were there to serve the interests of the Church.

Apart from office equipment, he also started a farm in Lundazi as an income generating activity for the Church. This farm was neglected soon after he left and now other people within Lundazi have occupied the place. However, through the current office the idea of the Church having a farm has been reconsidered by starting a farm in Chunga where the General Secretary resides, while another farm is in Chasefu. Still in Chasefu, the church in Zambia has also set up a Theological College, which shows the growth of the church. Jele was doing all these because he wanted the Church to be "self-governing, self-propagating and self-supporting"[99] as

---

[97] Interview Dr Jele, *Etchiyeni village, Mphongo,* 20.5.2009.

[98] Interview Rev Dr V Chilenje, Lundazi, 19.7.2009.

[99] Jack Thompson, *African Leadership in the Livingstonia Mission 1875-1900*, p. 88.

argued by the early missionaries who had accepted Henry Venn's concept.[100]

Although he had put up the above projects there was some opposition from some members. To most of the developments he was doing there were a lot of opposition, because people by then did not know where the Church was being driven. Some tried to prevent him in some programmes, but he forged ahead and managed to put up so many things. That is why the suggestion is that if a leader does not have opposition that leader becomes an idle leader thinking that all is perfect. Thus, in every institution there is need to have some opposition in order to come up with the ways that will help in overcoming the problems that the church is going through. This could be the reason why Ncozana argues that Jonathan Sangaya's problems while he was the first Malawian general secretary of Blantyre CCAP seen from a different angle were a blessing to Sangaya's leadership.[101]

Jele was also instrumental in the committee that was commissioned to do everything possible in readiness for the establishment of the CCAP Synod of Zambia despite having only two presbyteries. Although some of the projects he initiated did not appear to be important at first, when Jele left Zambia people began to realize that he had been very instrumental in establishing and developing the CCAP Synod of Zambia. The Bemba of Zambia have this saying: *Uwakwensha ubushiku bamutasha elyo bwacha.* (The one who guides you in the night is praised when it is dawn). This simply means that you will not praise the person who guides you now because you do not know how that person is guiding you. For instance, one will not even realize that where he is passing through there are many problems, but when the leader is gone, he will see and praise that leader. This is what most of the members in the CCAP Synod of Zambia have gone through, because after Jele had gone they realized that what he had been was doing was the right thing.

Jele's Legacy

What I have related so far shows that really there was something about this man of God; this is why the Zambian CCAP members could remember him. They remember Jele because he was a man who wanted the best and

---

[100] For more on their concept see: Stephan Neill, *A History of Christian Missions*, 2nd rev ed by Owen Chadwick, London, Penguin, 1990, pp. 220-221.

[101] Silas S. Ncozana, p. 35.

always wanted to make sure that all things around him were at best. For example, he ensured that elders in his congregation looked acceptable and presentable during Church services and any other major activities. He also made sure that the surroundings of the mission station were kept clean. Some remember him because of being a cheerful, well-equipped teacher with elderly skills. He worked very hard to see the Synod develop, that is why he came up with many developments when he was in the office. Jele is also remembered for being the first General Secretary who made sure that the Church grows and becomes a self-supporting one. He is also remembered because of his activeness, accountability and transparency, integrity and innovation, and therefore he was also able to find partners during his time.[102] Although his successors to a lesser extent made some significant contributions, they did not succeed in establishing partnerships. However, some later General Secretaries emulated some of his leadership skills in establishing partners with overseas churches, for instance, the Romans One Eleven Trust and the Presbyterian Church of Australia (PCA). Jele is remembered because he was a principled man who never tolerated laziness and who was ready to die for Christ.

Jele was educative and encouraging, fatherly and elderly, a man of God with good ideas. He is also remembered because he fought for the Synod of Zambia to be with the name of today. Some were suggesting that it be "Synod of Lundazi," but Jele and other colleagues argued that that would limit the Synod because Zambia was a wide country, so he promoted a name that would cater for all the Provinces in Zambia.

People say that where there is a successful man there is always a successful woman. This paper certainly agrees with them that, yes, at times it is so, because Jele's successes also at times depended on his wife. This is because about three quarters of the people interviewed said that Jele's wife really helped him to be the man he was. For example, Mr Mtambo of Chilenje had this to say, "Jele's wife was spirit-filled and when she preached one could feel that really, she was an anointed woman of God and that Jele was with us, this is not seen in some of the minister's wives."[103] His wife was a very good teacher who taught both men and women how to live in their homes and how to take care of their wives, husbands and children. Of this, most elders have argued that nowadays ministers' wives are not doing as much as we expect them to do. Some are not welcoming and very few entertain their visitors as Mrs. Jele used to do.

---

[102] Interview Dr Victor Chilenje, Lundazi, 20.7.2009.

[103] Interview Mr. Mtambo, Chilenje, Lusaka, 14.7.2009.

Therefore, this is a plea to current ministers to encourage their wives to participate in most of the church activities by being welcoming to the visitors. Jele was also good at exchanging visits both within and outside Zambia. In short, Jele has left a special legacy for today's leaders and members within the church and other institutions because of his productive and innovative skills. He was a parent to depend on and a teacher one can learn from. This is why upcoming leaders have to learn to be humble, respectful and hardworking. His aim in evangelism was to help people to know Christ as their personal saviour and as the one they can depend on. He was also a leader who needed the help of other people and advice from other people in order to carry out his duties effectively. As upcoming leaders, we as well need to seek advice from other people and analyze critically and then come up with concrete decisions. This could be the reason why Jele is remembered as a principled man who never tolerated laziness and that he was ready to die for Christ.

CONCLUSION

As we have seen in the previous chapters Jele was destined to become one of the influential leaders because of the legacy he has left in the CCAP Synod of Zambia. His services as a Parish Minister in the CCAP Synod of Zambia were some of the services that the CCAP members in Zambia will never forget. Thus, it is important to note that a leader should strive to be remembered, not for his glory but for God's glory. Throughout this study, one can see that Jele was prepared to sacrifice his life for the service he rendered to the CCAP in Zambia. His way of leadership shows his character of genuine commitment and calling. He did his work in a good manner and proved it by being able to communicate with all people, no matter who they were. His legacy goes beyond even what he did in Zambia. We can now see that he was a man standing in the gap at a crucial point in the history of the church in Zambia. The church was new and it had many challenges, but it was there that Jele and his companions took their stand clinging to biblical truth, resisting defeatism and striving to change the heart of the church. Jele's evangelistic sermons also touched the heart of the people through the language, expressions, idioms, parables and illustrations he was using.

Although Jele retired and returned home to Malawi after serving the Zambian Synod, he is still visible in Zambian memories. The mark he left is still shaping our minds in all aspects of life. This prompts us to contend that the Zambian CCAP church leaders cannot flourish in their leadership if they do not learn from Jele's leadership style. A good leader like Jele should be principled, determined, broadminded, innovative and instrumental in spearheading church projects and able to project the future of the church. The motive of being elected to the high office of the church should not aim at serving the self but serving others as Jele did.

Thus, Jele was instrumental in developing the CCAP church in Zambia, even though it was a young church. He is remembered and respected in the CCAP Synod of Zambia not only as a missionary but also as one who started to develop the church. It is where it is now because of some of his contributions. This could be the reason the Synod regularly extends her invitations to Jele to attend the Synod meetings because he is still part of the Church. The sense of belongingness and identity between Jele and the Synod of Zambia is strong and is that which is described in Genesis 2:23 – bone of my bone and flesh of flesh. It is a bond of relationship that enables the Synod of Zambia to continue to learn from Jele, although he is a retiree and away from them.

Based on the findings in this book, the following are some points that we as current church leaders can learn from Jele.

- Primarily the church and young leaders have to be productive and industrious, that is being good farmers who grow crops and keep animals like goats, cattle and pigs, rather than only waiting for others to come and do the work for us, because Jele was one man who never tolerated laziness, even up to now. He was a hard-working person.

- Apart from being productive, the church and future leaders have to be spiritually mature through prayers and the fellowship with our fellow parishioners and we must learn to be humble, respectful and hard working. Still further, we have to be fearless, focused, and should always aim at doing the best.

- Sustainability of one's vision is not only paramount but also the heart of the life of the church. Therefore, as new leaders we need to continue and improve where others have stopped. In doing this we have to examine critically what others have been doing and then, after analyzing that critically, find new ways on how we can improve where others have stopped.

- As a church and new leaders, we should not try to build a ministry until we have first built a relationship, and if that means rearranging our priorities, then we have to do it. The bible tells us that Jesus called the disciples to be with him, and then He sent them out from Him. We should not try to go out for Jesus, until we have first spent time with him. We have to be born again and develop our relationship with our Lord Jesus Christ.

- As a church and new leaders, we have to know that success in God's ministry is doing what we are supposed to do (Luke 17:10).

- As a church and new leaders, we have to be good in public relations. To be good in public relations one has to develop time to be with people so that he/she can know them. Seriousness, dedication to duty in the Church, and self-denial of earthly riches are also important and that is what God wants from us.[104]

- When reading this book, please do not only read about the life and work of Jele but learn something from this man. Does not Paul warn us in 1 Corinthians 10:1–13 that we have to learn from others as leaders and believers?

- As a church and new leaders, we are ambassadors for Christ (2 Corinthians 5:20). Indeed, an ambassador holds a position of great honour and responsibility. Thus, we have to know the mind of our King Lord Jesus Christ and present His own interest only, as we have learnt from Jele's life. This is because someone who follows his own opinions would never qualify to work in God's Kingdom.

- As a church and new leaders, we also have to know that we are living Bibles as we live and lead others (2 Corinthians 3:2). Therefore, as leaders and believers we have to be careful how we live today. We may be the only sermon someone will ever hear.

- Finally, but not the least, God will use whatever we have got. We should never try to be who we are not, but we should let God use us the way we are. In Exodus 4:2 God asked Moses, "What is in your hand?" Moses replied with a discouragement, "a staff". This staff was natural to Moses. Thus, God will use whatever we have got in our life naturally. Jele was used by God through what God gave him naturally. Even today God can use us naturally and the only secret is to make ourselves available. We should not try to be someone else,

---

[104] This could be the reason why Dr Chilenje argues that, "true leadership is one that depends only on God" (Interview Dr Chilenje, Lundazi, 19.7.2009).

but we have to discover who we are. Instead of comparing ourselves with others or try to change what God has made us to be, we must recognize the gifts we have got and start building on them.

Thus, as the church, new leaders and all of us who will read this book, we have to depend upon God in all we do if we are to prosper just as Jele did. Let us also learn something from this man of God, not just read about his life and work. Above all, we have to learn to suffer for Christ and die for him if we are to succeed.

T o God be the Glory.

Appendix

Offices and Achievements

- Moderator of Loudon – Chasefu Presbytery, 1969 to 1970
- Moderator of the CCAP Synod of Livingstonia 1979 to 1980
- First Full Time Evangelism Secretary of the CCAP Synod of Livingstonia, 1980 to 1981
- First Moderator of Lusaka – Copperbelt Presbytery, Zambia 1982 to 1983
- First General Secretary of CCAP Synod of Zambia, 1984 to 1988
- Moderator of Chasefu Presbytery, Zambia 1985 to 1986 (While working as the General Secretary of the CCAP Synod of Zambia)
- Moderator of Loudon Presbytery, Malawi 1989 to 1990 (after returning from Zambia)

World Conferences Attended by Dr Jele

- Evangelism Tour and Conferences in Birmingham, England, 1974
- Pan Africa Leadership Conference in 1976 in Nairobi, Kenya[105]
- Extensive Evangelism Conference "Love Africa" in Blantyre, Malawi 1978
- General Assembly of the Church of Scotland and Northern Ireland 1979 (where Rev. Dr Jele and Rev. W.P. Chibambo found funds for the Synod Offices in Mzuzu Headquarters.)
- Extensive Evangelism Course and Conference in Singapore 1981 (Diploma Conferred)
- International Conference for Itinerant Evangelists, Amsterdam, Netherlands 1983.[106]

---

[105] For a full record of the conference see: Michael Cassidy and Gottfried Osei-Mensah, *Together in One Place. The Story of PACLA, December 9-19, 1976*, Kisumu: Evangel, 1978; Michael Cassidy and Luc Verlinden, *Facing the New Challenges. The Message of PACLA, December 9-19, 1976*. Kisumu: Evangel, 1978.

[106] socialarchive.iath.virginia.edu4/ark/99166/w61s4w5k.

Moderators

From 1984 to date the following Ministers have served as Moderators of CCAP Synod of Zambia:

1984 – 1986	Rev. S. M. Mithi
1986 – 1988	Rev. N. M. Mtonga
1988 – 1990	Rev. S. M. Mithi
1990 – 1992	Rev. L. R. Mbewe (Late)
1992 – 1994	Rev. C. T. Soko
1994 – 1996	Rev. D. Tembo
1996 – 1998	Rev. F. J. Mwanza
1998 – 2000	Rev. L. Kalua
2000 – 2002	Rev. L. Nyirenda
2002 – 2004	Rev. D. Tembo
2004 – 2006	Rev. L. Nyirenda
2006 – 2008	Rev. Dr V. Chilenje
2008 – 2010	Rev. D. Tembo
2010 – 2012	Rev. Dr V. Chilenje
2012 – 2014	Rev. C. Chunda

General Secretaries

From 1984 to date the following Ministers has served as General Secretary of CCAP Synod of Zambia:

1984 – 1988	Rev. Dr W.M.K. Jele
1988 – 1989	Rev. F. J. Mwanza
1989 – 1992	Rev. S. M. Mithi
1992 – 2000	Rev. D. Chiboboka
2000 – 2004	Rev. Dr V. Chilenje
2004 – 2008	Rev. L. R. Mbewe (Late)
2008 – 2016	Rev. M. R. Kabandama

Deputy General Secretaries

From 1984 to date the following Ministers have served as Deputy General Secretary of CCAP Synod of Zambia:

1984 – 1988	Rev. F. J. Mwanza
1988 – 1992	Rev. D. Chiboboka
1992 – 1996	Rev. Dr V. Chilenje
1996 – 2000	Rev. D. Tembo
2000 – 2004	Rev. D. Chiboboka
2004 – 2008	Rev. L. Kaluah
2008 – 2016	Rev. G. Phiri

General Treasurers

From 1984 to date the following Elders has served as General Treasures of the CCAP Synod of Zambia:

1984 -1989	Mr. L. V. Zimba
1989 – 1992	Mr. H. Ngulube
1992 – 2003	Mr. E. L. Katyetye
2003 – To date	Mr. I. B. Ngulube

BIBLIOGRAPHY

Interviews

Personal interview with Rev Dr Wyson Moses Kauzobafa Jele, Etchiyeni village, Mphongo, Mzimba 20-05-09.

Personal interview with Mr B.K. Mbewe, Matero, Lusaka, 09-07-09

Personal interview with Rev Kondwani Nkhoma, Mandevu, 13-07-09

Personal interview with Rev S.M. Mithi, Kayama, Lusaka, 14-07-09

Personal interview with Mr Thompson Mtambo, Chilenje, Lusaka, Zambia, 14-07-09

Personal interview with Mr Ngwata, Kayama, Lusaka, 15-07-09

Personal interviews with the Rev Dr Victor Chilenje, Lundazi, 19-07-09 and 19-12-09

Personal interview with Rolina Ngwira, Lundazi, Zambia, 19- 07-09

Personal interview with Mr Chima, Lundazi, Zambia, 20-07-09

Telephone interview with Mr Wyson Mkochi, Lundazi, Zambia, 13-08-09

Telephone interview with the General Secretary, Rev M.R. Kabandama, 04-11-09

Unpublished

Chilenje, Victor, The Origin and Development of the Church of Central Africa Presbyterian (CCAP) in Zambia *1882-2004*, PhD, Stellenbosch University, 2007.

Kawamba, Bright, The Blantyre Spiritual Awakening 1969 to 1986: An Antecedent of the Charismatic Movement in Malawi, MA, University of Malawi, 2013.

Khonje, Boston, The Establishment, Growth and Contribution of the Student Christian Organization of Malawi (SCOM) to the Malawian Society 1961-2012, MA, Mzuzu University, 2013.

Minutes of General Synod of the Church of Central Africa Presbyterian 1987.

Minutes of Synod meeting of CCAP Synod of Zambia, 1984

Minutes of the General Synod of the Church of Central Africa Presbyterian 1964.

Published

Bosch, David, *Transforming Mission*, Maryknoll, New York: Orbis Books, 1991.

Cassidy, Michael and Gottfried Osei-Mensah, *Together in One Place. The Story of PACLA, December 9-19, 1976*, Kisumu: Evangel, 1978.

Cassidy, Michael and Luc Verlinden, *Facing the New Challenges. The Message of PACLA, December 9-19, 1976.* Kisumu: Evangel, 1978.

Green, Bryan, *The Practice of Evangelism*, London: Hodder and Stoughton, 1958.

Joyner, Rick, *Leadership, the Power of a Creative Life*, Fort Mill: Morning Star Publications, 2007.

Law, Robert, *Reminiscences of Livingstonia,* Edinburgh: Oliver and Boyd, 1934.

McCracken, John. *Politics & Christianity in Malawi 1875-1940*, Blantyre: CLAIM, [2]2000.

McPherson, F. "The 1959 Emergency at Livingstonia" *in Bulletin of the Scottish Institute of Missionary Studies,* No 10, 1994.

Ncozana, Silas, *Sangaya. A Leader in the Synod of Blantyre Church of Central Africa Presbyterian*, Blantyre: CLAIM, 1999.

Posner, Z. Barry and James M. Kouzes, *Leadership Challenge, third Edition,* San Francisco: Jossy-Bass, 2002.

Sanders, J. Oswald, *Spiritual Leadership: Principles of Excellence for Every Believer,* Chicago: Moody Press, 1994.

Selfridge, Jack, *Jack of all Trades Mastered by One,* Evanton, Christian Focus Publications, 1996.

Thompson, T. Jack, "African Leadership in Livingstonia Mission 1875-1900," in *Journal of Social Science,* Vol. II, 1973.

Thompson, T. Jack, *Christianity in Northern Malawi*, Leiden: Brill, 1995.

Weller, John and Jane Linden, *Mainstream Christianity to 1980 in Malawi, Zambia and Zimbabwe*, Gweru: Mambo Press, 1984.

Young, E.D., Mission to Nyassa, Journal of Adventures. John Murray. London: 1877.

Printed in the United States
By Bookmasters